LEARNING

MACHINE

From Data Science To Data Quality: When An Algorithm
Includes A Company's Performance In The Digital Age

TOMMASO MAZZIOTTI

TABLE OF CONTENTS

Introduction

You probably already have a pretty good idea of what machine learning is, but maybe the explanations you've gotten are just a little bit cloudy. You know it's a key component of artificial intelligence, but even that definition is a little fuzzy. It can be very difficult to wrap your head around the concept. It helps to understand that the foundation of machine learning lies firmly rooted in our own biology.

For eons, we've viewed the human brain as the only creation with the ability to learn and process information from complex data. Now, we're told that inanimate objects can learn and change their behavior through this innovation. It boggles the mind to think of it that way. However, there is a good reason why it is not only possible, but it is already a major part of how we live and do business today.

What Is It?

To put it in the simplest of terms, machine learning is the art of computer programming that allows the computer to learn and to automatically adjust its functions to perfect how well they accomplish their task. A computer with machine learning capabilities can actually improve their performance based on their own experience without having an explicit program to tell them exactly what to do.

This process of learning actually begins with the ability of the program to observe collected data and compare it with previous data to find patterns and results and adjust itself accordingly. All of this is done through a complex system of neural networks and algorithms working together in order to produce the desired results. In essence, it means that computers are slowly beginning to learn to think like humans, learning from their experiences and changing in order to improve the results they pick up.

It is now one of the most effective means of simplifying work that has to be done. By reducing the need for every program to be written for every possible function a machine can do, it allows the machine to teach itself how to perform the work done in a faster and more efficient manner.

If you're not quite sure how this works, let's use an example. Suppose you need to create a program that requires the computer to filter out certain types of data. In the traditional programming method, you would have to: 1) Have a human examine what data you want to be eliminated and then compile a list of ways that unwanted data might appear and identify the specific patterns that may appear. 2) Then the human would have to write a specific algorithm created to teach the computer exactly what to look for. 3) The human would then have to develop a software program that could identify those patterns and other details and label them accordingly. 4) Test the program and find any anomalies that could create a problem in finding the unwanted data and then go back to step one and repeat the process over and over again until the program is actually perfected.

Even with this pretty basic list of steps, you would only be able to program the computer to complete one task and would have to repeat the process for any other task that you also may need the computer to do. To complete all of these tasks, you will have to comply with an extensive list of rules in order for it to work correctly. This leaves your programming efforts open to errors popping up and disrupting the whole process. However, if you had chosen to use machine learning to accomplish the same thing, the process would have been done much more quickly with less risk of errors developing.

In addition, once the program is updated using the traditional method, the designer of the program could never feel like the job is done. He (or she) will always have to periodically go back and update it on a regular basis to ensure that it is compatible with the latest technology being used at the time. This would have to be done repeatedly until it is replaced by another program altogether.

Machine learning is a technique that, once uploaded, will run itself. It will automatically tell when updates need to be made and can even latch onto a system and get its own updates, freeing up the human to do other things. Machine learning makes it possible to solve even the most complex problems with minimal human interference. Depending on the type of machine learning you use, once it is live and active in the system, the machine can continue to make its own adjustments and recognize its own failures and successes for as long as it remains that way.

There are many advantages to using machine learning in computer programming today, but no doubt there will be many more new ways to use it in the future. Right now, it is primarily used to:

- Solve problems that involve long lists of rules
- Solve very complex problems that do not have any apparent solution
- Adapt to new data in non-stable environments

As more and more people become aware of how great machine learning can be, it is likely that it will be used in hundreds or thousands of other purposes. In time, it is feasible that it will be used in every industry in existence and may be used at some point to even create new ones.

CHAPTER 1:

Introduction to Machine Learning

Machine learning is what computers do, which comes naturally to people: learn from experience. Machine learning algorithms use computational procedures to "find out" information straight from the material without relying upon a predetermined equation for a model. Their functionality adaptively improves as the number of samples for learning rises out there. Education is a kind of machine learning.

Machine learning is a program of artificial intelligence (AI) that supplies systems the capability to learn and improve in expertise without being explicitly programmed automatically.

The method of learning starts with information or observations, such as immediate experience examples, or education, to make better choices in the future we supply and to search for patterns in data. The intention is to permit the computers to adapt actions and to understand them without human intervention.

Machine learning is used by many to improve advanced living. It includes procedures that are professional but also industrial. However, what is machine learning? It's a subset of artificial intelligence, which concentrates on using statistical approaches to find out from databases to construct computer systems. Machine learning is used in businesses and disciplines like medical investigation, picture processing, prediction, classification, learning institution, regression, etc.

Machine learning is one of the most influential technologies in the world today. We are far from viewing its entire potential. There is no doubt; it is going to continue to be creating headlines for the future. The following guide is designed as an introduction with no too large level, covering all of the basic ideas.

The majority of us are unaware that we interact with machine learning every moment. Each time we Google something, hear a tune or even have a picture, machine learning is getting a part of the motor behind it, always learning and progressing from each interaction. It is also behind improvements that are world-changing like self-driving cars, producing new medications, and discovering cancer.

Types of Machine Learning

Supervised Machine Learning

"Supervised machine learning" is widely used in predictive big data analysis because they are able to assess and apply the lessons learned from iterations and interactions to new data set. These learning algorithms are capable of labeling all their current events based on the instructions provided to efficiently forecast and predict future events. For example, the machine can be programmed to label its data points as "R" (Run), "N" (Negative), or "P" (Positive). The machine-learning algorithm then labels the input data as programmed and gets the correct output data. The algorithm compares the production of its own with the "expected or correct" output, identifies potential modifications, and resolves errors to make the model more accurate and smarter. By employing methods like "regression," "prediction," "classification," and "boosting of ingredients" to properly train the learning algorithms, any new input data can be fed to the machine as "target" data set to assemble the learning program as desired. This jump-starts the analysis and propels the learning algorithms to create an "inferred feature," which can be used to generate forecasts and predictions based on output values for future events. Financial organizations and banks, for example, depend heavily on machine-learning algorithms to track credit card fraud and foresee the likelihood of a potential customer not making their loan payments on time.

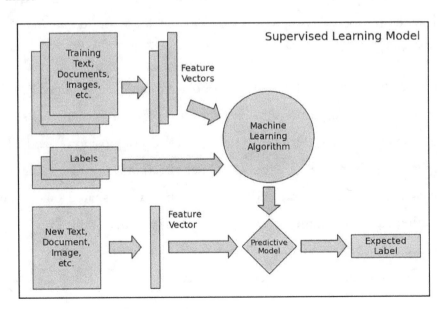

Unsupervised Machine Learning

Companies often find themselves in a situation in which data sources are required to generate a labeled and categorized training data set are unavailable. In these conditions, the use of unsupervised machine learning is ideal.

"Unsupervised learning algorithms" are commonly used to describe how the machine can produce "inferred features" to illustrate hidden patterns from an unlabeled and unclassified component in the stack of data.

These algorithms can explore the data so that a structure can be defined within the data mass. Although the unsupervised machine learning algorithms are as effective as the supervised learning algorithms in the exploration of input data and drawing insights from it, the unsupervised algorithms are not capable of identifying the correct output.

These algorithms can be used to define data outliers; to produce tailor-made product suggestions; to classify text topics using techniques such as "self-organizing maps," "singular value decomposition," and "k-means clustering." Customer identification, for example, customers can be segmented into groups with shared shopping attributes and targeted with similar marketing strategies and campaigns. Consequently, unsupervised learning algorithms are very common in the online marketing industry.

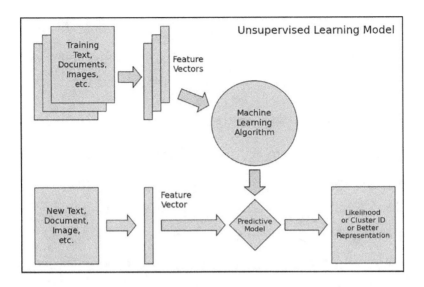

Semi-Supervised Machine Learning

The "semi-supervised machine learning algorithms" are extremely flexible and able to learn from "labeled" as well as "unlabeled" or raw data. These algorithms are a "hybrid" of supervised and unsupervised ML algorithms. Usually, the training data set consists of predominantly unlabeled data and a tiny portion of labeled data. The use of analytical methods such as the "forecast," "regression," and "classification" in combination with semi-controlled learning algorithms allows the computer to improve its accuracy in learning and training significantly. These algorithms are often used when the production of processed and labeled training data from the raw data set is highly resource-intensive and less cost-effective for the company. Companies are using their systems with semi-supervised learning algorithms to prevent additional personnel and equipment expenses. For example, the application of technology for "facial recognition" requires an enormous quantity of facial data dispersed across multiple input

14

sources. The processing, classification, and labeling of raw data obtained from sources, including internet cameras, requires a lot of resources and thousands of hours to be used as a training data set.

Reinforcement Machine Learning

Such algorithms perform activities and carefully record the results of each action, either as an error for a failed outcome or a reward for excellent results. The two main characteristics that distinguish the reinforcement learning algorithm are the "trial and error" analysis technique and the "delayed reward" feedback loop. The computer continually analyzes input data using a variety of calculations and transmits a signal of reinforcement for each correct or intended output to eventually optimize the final results. The algorithm creates an easy action and rewards feedback loop for assessing, recording, and learning what activity has been efficient, in that it resulted in right or intended output in a shorter time span. The use of such algorithms enables the system to determine optimal conduct automatically and to maximize its effectiveness in a specific context. Therefore, in the disciplines of gaming, robotics, and navigation systems, the reinforcement machine-learning algorithms are heavily utilized. The machine learning algorithms have proliferated to hundreds and thousands and counting.

Importance of Machine Learning

The seemingly unstoppable interest in ML stems from the same variables that have made "data mining" and "Bayesian analysis" more common than ever before. The underlying factors contributing to this popularity are increasing quantities and data varieties, cheaper and more effective computational processing, and inexpensive data storage. To get a sense of how significant machine learning is in our everyday lives, it is simpler to state what part of our cutting edge way of life has not been touched by it. Each aspect of human life is being impacted by the "smart machines" intended to expand human capacities and improve efficiencies. Artificial Intelligence and machine learning technology is the focal precept of the "Fourth Industrial Revolution" that could possibly question our thoughts regarding being "human."

All of these factors imply that models that can analyze larger, more complicated data while delivering highly accurate results in a short period of time can be produced rapidly and automatically on a much larger scale. Companies can easily identify potential growth opportunities or avoid unknown hazards by constructing desired machine learning models that meet their business requirements. Data runs through the vein of every company. Increasingly, data-driven strategies create a distinction between winning or losing the competition. Machine learning offers the magic of unlocking the importance of business and customer data to lead to actionable measures and decisions that can skyrocket a company's business and market share.

Machine learning has demonstrated over the recent years that many distinct tasks can be automated, which were once deemed as activities only people could carry out, such as image recognition, text processing, and gaming. In 2014, machine learning and AI professionals believed the board game "Go" would take at least ten years for the machine to defeat its greatest player in the world, but they were proved mistaken by "Google's DeepMind," which showed that machines are capable of learning which moves to take into account even in such a complicated game as "Go." In the world of gaming, machines have seen many more innovations such as "Dota Bot" from the "OpenAI" team. Machine learning is bound to have enormous economic and social impacts on our day to day lives. A complete set of work activities and the entire industrial spectrum could potentially be automated, and the labor market will be transformed forever.

Repetitive Learning Automation and Information Revelation

Unlike robotic automation driven by hardware that merely automates manual tasks, machine learning continuously and reliably enables the execution of high quantity, high volume, and computer-oriented tasks. Artificial intelligence machine-learning algorithms help to adapt the changing landscape by enabling a machine or system to learn, to take note of, and to reduce its previous mistakes. The machine learning algorithm works as a classifier or a forecasting tool to develop unique abilities and to define data patterns and structure. For instance, an algorithm for machine learning has created a model that will teach itself how to play chess and even how to create product suggestions based on consumer activity and behavioral data. This model is so effective because it can easily adjust to any new data set.

Machine learning allows the assessment of deeper and wider data sets by means of neural networks comprising several hidden layers. Just a couple of years ago, a scheme for detecting fraud with countless hidden layers would have been considered a work of imagination. A whole new world is on the horizon with the emergence of big data and unimaginable computer capabilities. The data on the machines is like the gas on the vehicle; more data addition leads to faster and more accurate results. Deep learning models thrive with a wealth of data because they benefit from the information immediately. The machine-learning algorithms have led to incredible accuracy through the "deep neural networks." Increased accuracy is obtained from deep learning, for instance, from the regular and extensive use of smart technology such as "Amazon Alexa" and "Google Search." These "deep neural networks" also boost our healthcare sector. Technologies like image classification and the recognition of objects are now able to detect cancer with the same precision as a heavily qualified radiologist on MRIs.

Artificial intelligence enables the use of big data analytics in combination with the algorithm for machine learning to be enhanced and improved. Data has developed like its own currency and can readily become "intellectual property" when algorithms are self-learning. The crude information is comparable to a gold mine in that the more and more you dig, the more you can dig out and extract "gold" or meaningful insights. The use of machine learning algorithms for the data allows the faster discovery of the appropriate solutions and can make these solutions more useful. Bear in mind that the finest data will always be the winner, even though everyone uses similar techniques.

CHAPTER 2:

Advantages of Machine Learning

D ue to the sheer volume and magnitude of the tasks, there are some instances where an engineer or developer cannot succeed, no matter how hard they try; in those cases, the advantages of machines over humans are clearly stark.

Identifies Patterns

When the engineer feeds a machine with artificial intelligence a training data set, it will then learn how to identify patterns within the data and produce results for any other similar inputs that the engineer provides the machine with. This is efficiency far beyond that of a normal analyst. Due to the strong connection between machine learning and data science (which is the process of crunching large volumes of data and unearthing relationships between the underlying variables), through machine learning, one can derive important insights into large volumes of data.

Improves Efficiency

Humans might have designed certain machines without a complete appreciation for their capabilities, since they may be unaware of the different situations in which a computer or machine will work.

Through machine learning and artificial intelligence, a machine will learn to adapt to environmental changes and improve its own efficiency, regardless of its surroundings.

Completes Specific Tasks

A programmer will usually develop a machine to complete certain tasks, most of which involving an elaborate and arduous program where there is scope for the programmer to make errors of omission. He or she might forget about a few steps or details that they should have included in the program. An artificially intelligent machine that can learn on its own would not face these challenges, as it would learn the tasks and processes on its own.

Helps Machines Adapt to the Changing Environment

With ever-changing technology and the development of new programming languages to communicate these technological advancements, it is nearly impossible to convert all existing programs and systems into these new syntaxes. Redesigning every program from its coding stage to adapt to technological advancements is counterproductive. At such times, it is highly efficient to use machine learning so that they can upgrade and adapt to the changing technological climate all on their own.

Helps Machines Handle Large Data Sets

Machine learning brings with it the capability to handle multiple dimensions and varieties of data simultaneously and in uncertain conditions. An artificially intelligent machine with abilities to learn on its own can function in dynamic environments, emphasizing the efficient use of resources.

Machine learning has helped to develop tools that provide continuous improvements in quality in small and larger process environments.

Disadvantages of Machine Learning

It is difficult to acquire data to train the machine. The engineer must know what algorithm he or she wants to use to train it, and only then can he or she identify the data set they will need to use to do so. There can be a significant impact on the results obtained if the engineer does not make the right decision.

- It's difficult to interpret the results accurately to determine the effectiveness of the machine-learning algorithm.
- The engineer must experiment with different algorithms before he or she chooses one to train the machine with.
- Technology that surpasses machine learning is being researched; therefore, it is important for machines to constantly learn and transform to adapt to new technology.

Subjects Involved in Machine Learning

Machine learning is a process that uses concepts from multiple subjects. Each of these subjects helps a programmer develop a new method that can be used in machine learning, and all these concepts together form the discipline of the topic.

Statistics

A common problem in statistics is testing a hypothesis and identifying the probability distribution that the data follows. This allows the statistician to predict the parameters for an unknown data set. Hypothesis testing is one of the many concepts of statistics that are used in machine learning. Another concept of statistics that's used in machine learning is predicting the value of a function using its sample values. The solutions to such problems are instances of machine learning since the problems in question use historical (past) data to predict future events. Statistics is a crucial part of machine learning.

Brain Modeling

Neural networks are closely related to machine learning. Scientists have suggested that nonlinear elements with weighted inputs can be used to create a neural network. Extensive studies are being conducted to assess these elements.

Adaptive Control Theory

Adaptive control theory is a part of this subject that deals with methods that help the system adapt to such changes and continue to perform optimally. The idea is that a system should anticipate the changes and modify itself accordingly.

Psychological Modeling

For years, psychologists have tried to understand human learning. The EPAM network is a method that's commonly used to understand human learning. This network is utilized to store and retrieve words from a database when the machine is provided with a function. In recent times, research in psychology has been influenced by artificial intelligence. Another aspect of psychology, called reinforcement learning has been extensively studied in recent times, and this concept is also used in machine learning.

Artificial Intelligence

As mentioned earlier, a large part of machine learning is concerned with the subject of artificial intelligence. Studies in artificial intelligence have focused on the use of analogies for learning purposes and on how past experiences can help in anticipating and accommodating future events. In recent years, studies have focused on devising rules for systems that use the concepts of inductive logic programming and decision tree methods.

Evolutionary Models

A common theory in evolution is that animals prefer to learn how to better adapt to their surroundings to enhance their performance. For example, early humans started to use the bow and arrow to protect themselves from predators that were faster and stronger than them. As far as machines are concerned, the concepts of learning and evolution can be synonymous with each other. Therefore, models used to explain evolution can also be utilized to devise machine learning techniques. The most prominent technique that has been developed using evolutionary models is the genetic algorithm.

Programming Languages

R

R is a programming language that is estimated to have close to 2 million users. This language has grown rapidly to become very popular since its inception in 1990. It is a common belief that R is not only a programming language for statistical analysis but can also be used for multiple functions. This tool is not limited to only the statistical domain. There are many features that make it a powerful language.

The programming language R is one that can be used for many purposes, especially by data scientists, to analyze and predict information through data. The idea behind developing R was to make statistical analysis easier.

As time passed, the language began to be used in different domains. There are many people who are adept at coding in R, although they are not statisticians. This situation has arisen since many packages are being developed that help to perform functions like data processing, graphic visualization, and other analyses. R is now used in the spheres of finance, genetics, language processing, biology, and market research.

Python

Python is a language that has multiple paradigms. You can probably think of Python as a Swiss Army knife in the world of coding since this language supports structured programming, object-oriented programming, functional programming, and other types of programming. Python is the second-best language in the world since it can be used to write programs in every industry and for data mining and website construction.

The creator, Guido Van Possum, decided to name the language Python, after Monty Python. If you were to use some inbuilt packages, you would find that there are some sketches of the Monty Python in the code or documentation. It is for this reason and many others that Python is a language that most programmers love, though engineers or those with a scientific background who are now data scientists would find it difficult to work with.

Python's simplicity and readability make it quite easy to understand. The numerous libraries and packages available on the internet demonstrate that data scientists in different sectors have written programs that are tailored to their needs and are available to download.

Since Python can be extended to work best for different programs, data scientists have begun to use it to analyze data. It is best to learn how to code in Python since it will help you analyze and interpret data and identify solutions that will work best for business.

CHAPTER 3:

Machine Learning Algorithms

Regression

I n the case of learning, you give illustrations that were known by definite. You state that for given characteristic worth x1, the output signal is y1, for x2 is y2, etc. According to this information, you allow the computer to determine an empirical connection between x and y.

When the system is trained in this manner with a sufficient amount of data points, you would ask the device to predict Y for a given X. Assuming you know the actual value of Y with this X, you'll have the ability to deduce if the machine's forecast is accurate.

You will test if the machine has discovered by utilizing the test information, when you're satisfied that the system can perform the predictions using a desirable level of precision (say 80 to 90 percent); you can stop additional coaching the machine.

You can use the system to perform on the predictions data request the machine to predict Y for a given X for which you don't know the worth of Y or points. This practice comes, we spoke.

Classification

You may utilize machine learning methods for classification issues. To one group, you categorize objects of character in classification problems. As an instance, in some 100 student's states, you might like to set them into three classes according to their peaks—short, medium, and extended-term. Assessing every student's height, you may place them at a group.

When a student comes in, you may put him within by measuring his height set. You'll train the system by following the principles from regression instruction. After the machine accomplishes forming the band, it is going to have the ability to classify any unknown new pupil correctly. You would use the evaluation data to confirm that the device has discovered your method of classification before placing the version that is developed in creation.

Where the AI started its supervised learning is a journey. This technique was implemented in many scenarios. You've used this version while doing precisely the hand-written recognition in your machine. Several algorithms are developed for learning that you are going to learn about them.

Generating Predictions Using Logistic Regression

Your training data should be used to approximate coefficients (beta values b) of the logistic regression algorithm. This is done with a maximum estimate of likelihood.

Maximum likelihood estimates are a common learning algorithm used by a variety of machine learning algorithms, but it does make assumptions about the distribution of your data.

The optimal equations will result in a formula that would estimate for the default class a value very near 1 (e.g., male) and for the other class a value very similar to 0 (e.g., female). The maximal logistic regression principle is that a scanning method searches for coefficient values (beta values), which decrease the error of the model-predicted probabilities of those in the data (i.e., the likelihood of 1 if the data is of the primary class). We won't go into the analysis of the highest chance. Suffice it to say that a minimization algorithm is used to optimize the best values for your training data's coefficients. This is usually done with an effective numerical optimization method (similar to the quasi-newton procedure).

If you are learning logistics, the much simpler gradient descent algorithm can implement it yourself from scratch.

Making Predictions With Logistic Regression

Predictions using a logistic regression model are just as straightforward as plugs in numbers and the estimation of a consequence into the logistic regression equation.

With a specific example, let's make this concrete.

Let's assume we have a model that can determine whether a person is male or female by height (full of fiction). The individual is male or female at a height of 150 cm.

The coefficients of b0= -100 and b1 = 0.6 have been learned. The above equation helps us to measure the likelihood of a person at or more formally P (male) provided 150 cm height. We will use EXP for example, as you can use it if you type this illustration into your tablet:

$$y = e^{\wedge} (b0 + b1*X) / (1 + e^{\wedge}(b0 + b1*X))$$

$$y = exp(-100 + 0.6*150) / (1 + EXP(-100 + 0.6*X))$$

$$y = 0.0000453978687$$

Or a near-zero likelihood that the individual is a man.

For reality, we will simply use the odds. Since that's classification and we want a limited response, for example, we may snap the probabilities into a binary class value:

0 if p(male) < 0.5

1 if p(male) >= 0.5

Now that we can use logistic regression to make predictions let us look at how we can plan our data to get the most out of this methodology.

Naïve Bayes Classifier

In a Naïve Bayes classifier, it is assumed that the availability of a certain feature in a certain class is not related to the presence of any other feature.

For example, an apple is a fruit with a diameter of about 3 cm, round, and red in color.

Although these features are dependent or rely on the presence of other features, their contributions to the probability of the fruit being an apple are independent.

Therefore, the classifier is called "naïve."

It's easy to build a Naïve Bayes model and use it with large datasets.

This classifier is also known to be good compared to the other classification algorithms.

The Naïve Bayes classifier predicts the membership probabilities of every class like the probability of a given data point or record belonging to a certain class.

The class that has the highest probability is the most likely class. This is also referred to as the Maximum a Posteriori (MAP).

How Does the Algorithm Work?

To understand how the Naïve Bayes Algorithm works, we can use an example.

Suppose we have a training data set about the weather and the target variable, which is "Play."

Our goal is to classify/determine whether players will or won't play depending on the weather condition.

The following steps can help you perform the classification:

Weather	Play
Sunny	No
Overcast	Yes
Rainy	Yes
Sunny	Yes
Sunny	Yes
Overcast	Yes
Rainy	No
Rainy	No
Sunny	Yes
Rainy	Yes
Sunny	No
Overcast	Yes
Overcast	Yes
Rainy	No

First, convert your dataset into a frequency table.

This is given below:

Frequency Table		
Weather	No	Yes
Overcast		4
Rainy	3	2
Sunny	2	3
Grand Total	5	9

Create a likelihood table simply by determining the probabilities, i.e., the overcast probability is 0.29, playing is 0.64.

Use the Naïve Bayes equation to determine the posterior probability for every class. A class with the highest probability will be the result of the prediction.

Suppose you have the following problem:

The players will play on sunny weather.

Your task is to determine whether the statement is correct or incorrect.

This problem can be solved using the posterior probability method as follows:

$$P(Yes \mid Sunny) = P(Sunny \mid Yes) * P(Yes) / P(Sunny)$$

We then have the following:

P(Sunny) = 5/14 = 0.36,

(Sunny | Yes) = 3/9 = 0.33,

P(Yes)= 9/14 = 0.64

Then,

P (Yes | Sunny) = 0.33 * 0.64 / 0.36 = 0.60

This shows it has a high probability.

In Naïve Bayes, the same approach is used for prediction of the probability of a different class depending on different attributes.

Pros of Naïve Bayes

- It is a fast, easy way to predict a class of data set for testing. It can also be applied very well in the prediction of a multi-class problem.

- When the assumption of independence is true, the Naïve Bayes classifier works very well compared to the other models. Much less training data is needed.

- It performs better when we have categorical input variables than numerical variables. For the case of numerical variables, we need to have an assumption that there is a normal distribution.

Cons of Naïve Bayes

- For a categorical variable with some category that hasn't been observed in the data set, the model assigns a zero-probability making it unable to generate a prediction. This is called a "Zero Frequency." The smoothing technique can be used to solve this problem. Laplace estimation can be employed to solve it.

- Naïve Bayes is referred to as a bad estimator. Sometimes the outputs it gives are not taken seriously.

- The Naïve Bayes also assumes the predictors are independent. In a real-life situation, it's nearly impossible for us to get independent predictors.

Applications of Naïve Bayes Algorithm

The Naïve Bayes Classifier is applied in the following fields:

Real-Time Prediction

Naïve Bayes is a faster learning classifier. This makes it applicable in making real-time predictions.

Multi-Class Prediction

- The Naïve Bayes Classifier is known to be good in multi-class prediction. We can use it for the prediction of target variables of multiple classes.

Text Classification/Sentiment Analysis/Spam Filtering

When used for text classification, Naïve Bayes Algorithm models give a high accuracy compared to the other types of models. It is also used in spam filtering to identify spam emails and in sentiment analysis, for example, in social media to determine positive as well as negative customer comments.

Recommendation Systems

The Naïve Bayes Classifier together with Collaborative Filtering can be used to build a recommendation system that uses data mining and machine learning techniques for filtering any unseen information. It can also generate a prediction on whether a user will like or reject a resource.

CHAPTER 4:

Neural Network Learning Models

A widely used approach in machine learning, the employment of artificial neural networks is inspired by the brain system of humans. The objective of neural networks is to replicate how the human brain learns. The neural network system is an ensemble of input and output layers and a hidden layer that transforms the input layer into useful information to the output layer. Usually, several hidden layers are implemented in an artificial neural network. The figure below presents an example of a neural network system composed of 2 hidden layers:

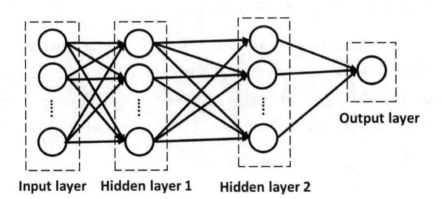

Input layer   Hidden layer 1   Hidden layer 2

Example of an Artificial Neural Network

Before going further and explaining how neural networks work, let's first define what a neuron is. A neuron is simply a mathematical equation expressed as the sum of the weighted inputs. Let's consider $X=\{x1, x2,....xM\}$ a vector of N inputs, the neuron is a linear combination of all inputs defined as follows:

$F(X=\{x1, x2,....xM\})=w1x1+w2x2+....+wMxM;$

With $w1, w2,...wM$ is the weights assigned to each input. The function F can also be represented as:

$F(X)=WX,$

With W a weight matrix and X a vector of data. The second formulation is very convenient when programming a neural network model. The weights are determined during the training procedure. In fact, training an artificial neural network means finding the optimal weights W that provide the most accurate output.

To each neuron, an activation function is applied the resulted weighted sum of inputs X. The role of the activation function is deciding whether the neuron should be activated or not according to the model's prediction. This process is applied to each layer of the network.

Components of Artificial Neural Networks

Neurons

The artificial neural network retained the biological resemblance of the brain in terms of receiving data through inputs, activation, processing, and delivering results using output functions. In computers, however, the information is usually external data, for example, images and files, which are then processed and provision of outputs through organizing and recognizing patterns in data. The neurons, therefore, play a significant role in providing a transition between the input and the output through the hidden layers.

Connections and Weights

Artificial neural networks have links that allow the transmission of information from one neuron to another. This henceforth facilitates the process of movement of data from the input to the hidden layers and the output. More so, each connection has its own weight assigned to it based on the importance of the neuron. In most cases, one neuron possesses several inputs and output connections with relatively varying weights. The pattern of relationship is usually referred to as its architecture, while the weight is determined in the form of algorithms, training, and learning processes involved in a given neural network.

Propagation Function

This is the function that calculates the input and output neuron as well as the predecessor neurons. The propagation function primarily facilitates the connections in relation to the weighted sum of the neural network at hand. In some cases, neurons may lack the capability of handling specific data, which are typically determined by these functions. The propagation function computes the relationship, effectiveness, and some complexity of data when transmitting from the input to the output with limited impact to the network.

What Are the Types of Artificial Neural Networks?

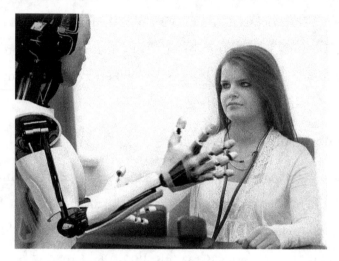

Several categories of artificial neural networks with different properties and complexities exist. The first and simplest neural network developed is the perceptron. The *perceptron* computes the sum of the inputs, applies an activation function, and provides the result to the output layer.

Another old and simple approach is the *feedforward neural network*. This type of artificial neural network has only one single layer. It is a category that is fully connected to the following layer where each node is attached to the others. It propagates the information in one direction from the inputs to the outputs through the hidden layer. This process is known as the front propagated wave that usually uses what is called the activation function. This activation function processes the data in each node of the layers. This neural network returns a sum of weights by the inputs calculated according to the hidden layer's activation function. The category of feedforward neural network usually uses the backpropagation method for the training process and the logistic function as an activation function.

Several other neural networks are a derivation of this type of network. For example, *the radial basis functions neural* network. This is a feedforward neural network that depends on the radial basis function instead of the logistic function. This type of neural network has two layers, wherein the inner layer, the features, and radial basis functions are combined. The radial function computes the distance of each point to the relative center. This neural network is useful for continuous values to evaluate the distance from the target value.

In contrast, the logistic function is used for mapping arbitrary binary values (i.e., 0 or 1; yes or no). *Deep feedforward neural networks* are a multilayer feedforward neural network. They became the most commonly used neural network types used in machine learning as they yield better results. A new type of learning called deep learning has emerged from this type of neural network.

Recurrent neural networks are another category that uses a different type of nodes. However, outputs of the hidden layers are saved and processed back to the previous layer. Basically, the first layer, comprised of the input layer, is processed as the product of the sum of the weighted features. It actually uses memory, while the computation is running. In other words, information is processed in two directions, unlike the feedforward neural networks.

A multilayer perceptron or multilayer neural network is a neural network that has at least three or more layers. This category of networks is fully connected, where every node is attached to all other nodes in the following layers.

Convolutional neural networks are typically useful for image classification or recognition. The processing used by this type of artificial neural network is designed to deal with pixel data. The convolutional neural networks are a multi-layer network that is based on convolutions, which apply filters for neuron activation. When the same filter is applied to a neuron, it leads to an activation of the same feature and results in what is called a feature map. The feature map reflects the strength and importance of a feature of input data.

Modular neural networks are formed from more than one connected neural network. These networks rely on the concept of 'divide and conquer.' They are handy for very complex problems because they allow combining different types of neural networks. Therefore, they allow combining the strengths of a different neural network to solve a complex problem where each neural network can handle a specific task.

How to Train an Artificial Neural Network?

As explained at the beginning, neural networks compute a weighted sum of inputs and apply an activation function at each layer. Then it provides the final result to the output layer. This procedure is commonly named as forward propagation. In order to train these artificial neural networks, weights need to be optimized to obtain the optimal weights that produce the most accurate outputs. The process of the training an artificial neural network is as follows:

- Initialize the weights
- Apply the forward propagation process
- Evaluate the neural network performance
- Apply the backward propagation process
- Update the weights
- Repeat the steps from step 2 until it attains a maximum number of iterations, or neural network performance does not improve

As we can see from the steps of training an artificial neural network presented above, we need a performance measure that describes how accurate the neural network is. This function is called the loss function or cost function.

$J = (1/N) * \sum (ypredicted - ytarget)2$

Where N: the number of outputs, *ypredicted*: the output and *ytarget*: the true value of the output. This function provides the error of the neural network. Small values of J reflect the high accuracy of the neural network.

So far, we defined loss function and how the neural network works in general. Now, let's go into the details for each step of the training process.

Let's consider a set of inputs X and outputs Y. We initialize W (i.e., weights) and B (i.e., bias) as a null matrix. The next step is to apply the feedforward propagation that consists of feeding each layer of the artificial neural network with the sum of the weights by the inputs and the bias. Let's consider that we have two layers. We can calculate the first hidden layer's output using the following equation:

$Z1=W1*X+b1$

Where W1 and b1 are the parameters of the neural network as the weights and bias of the first layer, respectively.

Next, we apply the activation function F1, that can be any activation from the function presented previously:

$A1=F1(Z1)$.

The result is the output of the first layer, which then is feed to the next layer as:

$Z2=W2*A1+b2$

W2 and b2 are the weights and bias of the second layer, respectively.

To this result, we apply an activation function F2:

A2=F2(Z2).

Now A2 is supposed to be the output of the artificial neural network. The activation function F1 and F2 might be the same activation function or different activation function depending on the dataset and the expected output.

After the feedforward propagation, we compare the neural network output against the target output with the loss function. It is highly likely the difference between the estimated output and the actual values at this stage is very high. Therefore, we have to adjust the weights through the backpropagation process. We calculate the gradient of each activation function concerning biases and weights. We start by evaluating the derivative of the last layer, then the layer before this layer on so on until the input layer. Then update the weights according to the gradient or the derivative of the activation function. Applying these steps to our example of two layers neural network it provides:

$W2=W2-\alpha*(dF2(W, b)/dW)$

$B2=b2- \alpha*(dF2(W, b)/db)$

$W1=W1-\alpha*(dF2(W, b)/dW)$

$B1=b1- \alpha*(dF2(W, b)/db)$

The parameter α is the learning rate parameter. This parameter determines the rate by which the weights are updated. The process that we just describe here is called the gradient descent algorithm. The process is repeated until it attains a pre-fixed maximum number of iterations. We will develop a classifier based on an artificial neural network.

CHAPTER 5:

What You Need to Know to
Get Started with Deep Learning

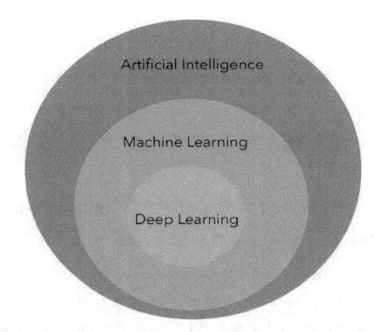

The innovations and breakthroughs that have been accomplished with deep learning are enough to get a lot of people excited about it. It is said that we live in the age of technology and with the many strides already achieved by deep learning; the next age will probably be the age of artificial intelligence. To that end, there will be more and more people looking to enter this field, so they can have a role in ushering in this new era.

However, before they can do that, there are a lot of things you must come to understand. Now that these fundamentals are so clearly realized, we will begin to see artificial intelligence emerge in all sorts of industries.

This is a complex field and for anyone to get a firm grasp on it, it helps to have a basic understanding of subjects like linear algebra, calculus, probability, and programming. If you don't have this background, it doesn't mean that you cannot grasp these concepts, but it does mean you'll have to do a little extra homework to get through the meat of it all.

You'll also need to know some practical differences in how deep learning differs and why it is so much more efficient than any other type of artificial intelligence before it.

Deep Learning, Machine Learning, Artificial Intelligence — What's the Difference

Often when you research deep learning, you'll come across several different terms that seem to be used interchangeably. Deep learning, machine learning, and artificial intelligence, while these are all related, there are some distinct differences that set them all apart from each other.

So, what exactly is deep learning? Basically, it is a type of machine learning that uses a system of neural networks that are designed to mimic the learning of the human brain. This network's focus is to simplify how a machine uses certain learning algorithms, which can be applied in artificial intelligence and machine learning. In fact, it is virtually impossible to have artificial intelligence without deep learning.

Because of deep learning, we now have the ability to develop massively large neural networks that have the ability to absorb information and respond to it without the need for a human to program its every move. The expectation is that one day, these machines will be able to operate autonomously, completely on their own without any form of human interference.

For the layperson, we are familiar with the term "artificial intelligence." It is the stuff of countless science fiction movies. However, few people understand that it is no longer science fiction but is definitely emerging in the realm of reality.

To explain:

Deep learning is a form of machine learning that is used to teach machines how to learn in a way that is similar to the learning process in the human brain.

Machine learning is a series of algorithms that give machines the ability to collect data, analyze it, and make decisions based on that analysis.

Artificial intelligence is a machine programmed with machine learning, so it can gather data and make decisions based on that data.

In its most basic form, deep learning is simply another type of machine learning. Basic machine learning has improved over the years and deep learning is the latest link in the evolutionary chain. In its early stages of development, deep learning machines were only capable of learning from data that had already been labeled and stored into the machine. This meant it could only function with human supervision. Unsupervised learning was still far into the future, but many believed it was a very real possibility. Now, machines can learn in all sorts of ways.

How a Machine Learns

When it comes to learning, we humans do it without any thinking or programming. Our minds have never had to be trained in how to learn something. From the time we're born, our five senses go immediately into action, collecting data and submitting it to our brains. Our brains process it, analyze it, and then make decisions based on it. If we're walking out at night, our brain automatically assesses the scene, determines a level of danger, and tells our feet to move faster. If we're watching a movie, our brain takes all that information in and determines whether we should cry, laugh, or be angry. We have what is called unsupervised learning. No one has to program those details and responses to us.

In addition, once we learn a concept, it then becomes a foundation from which we can build on. We first learn the alphabet (the initial concept) then we learn the sounds related to that alphabet, then we learn to string sounds together, creating words. Eventually, we'll be able to read and this is called layered learning. With that thought in mind, we can continue to build our knowledge base and grow from there.

The concept of machine learning is similar. While it is a far cry from doing the amazing things that a human brain can do, its function is based on a similar set of situations. A massive set of neural networks are created, each one communicating with the other. It also collects data and responds to the information it receives.

With artificial intelligence, the machine will be able to take in raw data and respond with a selection of pre-programmed responses. They will be able to "learn" from the data input and build on it. The major difference is that at present, machines can only learn from human input and develop their own concepts from the information gathered. This is one step closer to mimicking the human learning process.

Deep learning is basically a unique form of machine learning that is much more flexible than other previous forms used. By using a nested hierarchy of concepts, it can access many layers of non-linear information processing and achieve both supervised and unsupervised learning, which is ideal for pattern analysis and classification.

Deep neural networks consist of several layers called a hierarchical neural network. In this type of network, every layer has the ability to change its input data into something that is more abstract. The output layer will then combine the various features of input data and formulate a prediction. This method improves calculations, so it is much easier to understand.

While there are several different ways that machines can learn information, their strategies can be categorized into two separate classes. The first being supervised learning that uses labeled data to classify information. This form of learning is based on data that produces "expected answers." For example:

Visual Recognition

Imagine an AI designed to identify pedestrians walking across a street. It can be trained by inputting millions of short videos of street scenes collected. Some of the videos will have pedestrians walking while other videos will not. Some of the videos will have many people walking while some may have only one.

With a number of learning algorithms applied to the data, each giving the machine access to the correct answers, a variety of models are designed to teach the machine how to identify pedestrians in fast-moving scenes. The algorithms are tested against an unlabeled set of data that will check for accuracy.

Predictions

Supervised learning can also be used in making different predictions. A machine can be taught to estimate risk by inputting a large number of actual trades made by real investors and the results they received. It can then be asked to give an estimate of risk for each trade based on several fundamental factors of previous trades: price, volume, company, etc.

It then takes its estimated risk and compares it to the historical results during several different time intervals (day, week, month, and year) to determine if its predictions are accurate or within normal expectations.

Unsupervised learning works a little differently. The machine receives input without any related yield factors. The answers are derived purely from the calculations made. The goal of this type of learning is to demonstrate the basic structure or dissemination of the information so that the machine can gather even more details about the information. Unlike with supervised learning, the machine is not given any right answer and there is no human instructor guiding its data. The AI may collect the data and sort it according to its similarities or differences, even if there is no classification. The goal is to show a fundamental structure in the information in an effort to get a better understanding of it.

It is referred to as unsupervised learning because there is no instructor guiding it to the right conclusions. The machine will perform its own calculations in an effort to determine the nature of the data that it has collected.

While there are obvious advantages to unsupervised learning, there are still some problems it has yet to resolve. For example, a machine may be capable of identifying basic visual images (it can tell a cat from a dog) it may also end up creating new classifications in an attempt to distinguish between varying differences within a certain classification. It may not be able to tell a German shepherd from a Chihuahua. Its purpose is to find relationships within the data it receives, but this can create several problems when it tries to go further than that.

Clustering is when the AI attempts to decipher different groups within the data, whereas the association is an attempt to determine specific rules that will describe the data. Both of these can present huge problems in AI when their results are skewed by unanticipated groupings.

In reinforcement learning, the machine is trained to recognize activities. To come to this conclusion, it learns from its own actions and not from a human instructor giving it the necessary input. The goal, in this case, is not to make a classification or a prediction of events but instead to develop a policy of behavior.

We can find a perfect example of this in our relationship with household pets. If you're going to teach your dog a new trick, you can't just input the information and give it instructions on how you want it to behave. However, if you reward it for doing something and penalize it for other actions, eventually, the dog will learn how to do the things that give it rewards and avoid the behavior and those actions that bring on discipline.

Reinforcement learning in machines works in a similar way with a few differences.

- Substitute the pet with the machine
- Substitute the treat for a reward function
- Substitute the good behavior with a resultant action

In order for this to work, you need to have a feedback loop that will reinforce what the machine is actually learning. It is rewarded when it performs certain actions and is disciplined when it is wrong. You might wonder how you can reward or discipline a machine that has no feelings and no emotions. The system will work something like this:

- The machine is given an internal state that it must maintain. This state is used to learn about the environment.

- The reward function is used to teach the machine how to behave.

- The environment is the situation or scenario that the machine must operate in. It consists of all the things the agent can observe and respond to.

- The action is the behavior of the machine.

- The agent performs all the deeds.

CHAPTER 6:

Data Science Lifecycle and Technologies

Data Science Lifecycle

The data analyst is going to spend some time explaining what is going on because they are able to process the history that the data went through. On the other hand, the scientist of data is not only going to do exploratory analysis in order to figure out what insights are there, but they get the benefit of using some of the more advanced algorithms in machine learning in order to figure out how likely an event is going to happen in the future.

The data scientist is going to have a fun job at this. They are going to specifically take the time to look at the data from a lot of different angles, and some of these angles may be brand new, and ones that no one had considered in the past.

So, to keep it simple, data science is going to be used to help us make some predictions and decisions through a lot of different methods. And one of these methods is going to be through machine learning.

The Lifecycle of Data Science

Knowing what this is and how it works is going to make a big difference in the amount of success that you are able to get with this field, and it will help you to get the best results possible out of the process. Some of the steps that come with the data science lifecycle include:

Discovery

The first step that we need to explore is going to be the discovery. Before you begin any kind of project in this field, you will need to know the different properties, the requirements, the specifications, and the required budget. Otherwise, it is hard to know where you need to get started. Once you have a bit of this information in place, you will be able to do an assessment of the people, time, data, support, and technology to figure out if the project is something that you will be able to do. If you are short on any of those aspects, then it may be time to evaluate whether or not you would be able to do without them or get them before you start.

For this stage, you are going to need to take some time to do some research. You need to have a full understanding of the project you would like to do, and you need to know if you have the right resources to get all of it done. And if it is needed and the project is something that is necessary and you want to do it but without the right resources, you need to figure out what you can do to change this around.

Another thing that you are going to need to focus on when you are working in this stage is that you will need to frame the business problem that you want to fix and make better, while also formalizing that initiation hypothesis that you would like to be able to test.

Data Preparation

When you are done with the steps above, it is time to move on to the second stage. In this one, you are going to need some analysis to see results. You want to have a kind of analytical sandbox in order to perform the right analytics for the whole time that you are working on the project. You will need to explore, take some time to preprocess, and condition the data before you do the modeling.

Once you are done with some of those steps, it is time to go take this a bit further. You will need to do something known as ETLT. This stands for extract, transform, load, and transform. This allows you to get the data that you want into the sandbox so that you can do some of the experiments that you would like to do.

This is a great time for you to get the data all set up and ready to use. If you don't take the time to process through the data that you have in the proper manner, then it is going to be almost impossible for you to get the right algorithm, or to even be able to use it in the proper way either. Once you have been able to clean out the data and prepare it a bit, you can then go through and do what is known as exploratory analytics on it to learn more.

Model Planning

Once you have been able to clean and prepare any of the data that you would like to use in your models, it is time to actually plan out the models. In this third step, you are going to take some time to determine the proper techniques and models that you want to use in order to draw a good relationship between the variables. You will find, and we will talk about, a lot of different models that you can work with in order to see some separation and understanding of the data, but you need to pick the one that is right for you.

These relationships are important to find and define in the proper manner. These are basically going to set up the base that you need for any algorithm that you want to implement. You will then be able to apply the EDA or the Exploratory Data Analytics using a lot of different visualization tools and even statistical formulas, based on your own needs. There are a lot of different tools that you are able to choose to use for this, but R is going to be the one that is used the most. Once you have a bit of an insight into the nature of your chosen data, and you have taken that information to pick out the algorithm that you would like to use, it is the time to move on to stage four, where we are going to apply that chosen algorithm and built up a model to help us out.

Model Building

When we get to this phase, you will need to develop some sets of training and testing the data that you have. You first need to take a look at some of the tools that you already have and then decide if they are going to be enough for running the model that you want, or if you need an environment that is more robust. Depending on the kind of algorithm that you want to use, you may need to pick out something that is faster and needs to work with parallel processing instead.

When you are building up the model that you would like to use, remember that you are going to be using a lot of different techniques. Even though we spend some time splitting up the different algorithms that you are able to use with this kind of process, it is possible that you will use many tools to make your model. You could use different techniques like classification, clustering, and association, to build up the model.

Operationalize

Now, we need to move on to the fifth phase. In this one, you have had some time to create a model, use one or more algorithms, and bring in a few different tools. You should have your data organized and ready to use. When you get to this phase, you are going to be able to deliver everything from the technical documents, code documents, briefings, and final reports.

In addition to the things above, you are sometimes going to be able to implement a pilot project in a real-time production environment based on the information that you were able to get out of this data. This is a fun thing to do because you get a clear picture of how the performance of the algorithms and tools did. And it is all done on a small scale to figure out if they work and if there are any flaws before you deploy it through the whole business.

Communicate the Results

After you have had the time to present your findings and maybe deploy the model on a small scale, it is time to have some communication about whether or not this was able to achieve its goals. It is important for everyone to come together and really evaluate if they were able to achieve the goals that they set early on in the project.

This means that again you need to do some analysis of what you did throughout and check whether the final results were what you expected. In this last phase, you will need to identify the key findings that showed up, spend some time communicating what happened and how you came to those results with the stakeholders, and then determine whether the results that you saw in the project were a failure or a success based on the goals that you wanted to get in the beginning.

Everyone needs to come together during this phase and determine whether or not the results were what they thought. If they were completely off and no one is happy with them, then it is time to move on and try out something else instead. If it worked out, but some things were missing, it is time to see what adjustments can come into play to make it a bit better.

If the model worked the way that you want and there doesn't seem to be any glitches or issues that you need to fix up with it, then it is time to start making the goals that are needed in order to implement it throughout the whole business. This should be an exciting time because you have already seen the results that come with it working on a trial run. It is time to let it go free and see what results from, you are able to get overall.

Data science is an exciting part of the technology field, and it has been able to make some big changes to the way that many businesses are able to sort through and handle all of that data that is coming in on a regular basis. This helps them to learn more about how they run business, how the customers may react to some changes, and can make them more efficient and friendly.

Machine learning is going to help us to come up with some of the learning algorithms that you need in order to go through the data and recognize the patterns that will show up. We are going to spend some time looking at machine learning and all of the different types of algorithms and tools that come with it and this will help you to really see some amazing results.

CHAPTER 7:

Business Intelligence

What Is Business Intelligence?

Business intelligence (BI) is the gathering of techniques and apparatuses used to dissect business data. Business intelligence tasks are altogether increasingly compelling when they consolidate outside data sources with inward data hotspots for noteworthy understanding.

Business analytics, otherwise called progressed analytics, is a term regularly utilized conversely with business intelligence. Notwithstanding, business analytics is a subset of business intelligence since business intelligence manages methodologies and devices, while business analytics concentrates more on techniques. Business intelligence is distinct, while business analytics is increasingly prescriptive, tending to an issue or business question.

Aggressive intelligence is a subset of business intelligence. Focused intelligence is the accumulation of data, apparatuses, and forms for gathering, getting to, and dissecting business data on contenders. Aggressive intelligence is frequently used to screen contrasts in items.

Business Intelligence Applications in the Enterprise

Estimation

Numerous business intelligence instruments are utilized in estimation applications. They can take input data from sensors, CRM frameworks, web traffic, and more to gauge KPIs. For instance, answers for an offices group at an enormous assembling organization may incorporate sensors to quantify the temperature of key hardware to enhance support plans.

Analytics

Analytics is the investigation of data to discover significant patterns and bits of knowledge. This is a well-known use of business intelligence apparatuses since it enables businesses to deeply comprehend their data and drive an incentive with data-driven choices. For instance, a marketing association could utilize analytics to decide the customer sections well on the way to change over to another customer.

Revealing

Reportage is a standard utilization of business intelligence programming. BI items can now consistently produce normal reports for inward partners, mechanize basic undertakings for examiners, and trade the requirement for spreadsheets and word-processing programs.

For instance, a business activities examiner may utilize the instrument to create a week by week report for her chief itemizing a week ago's deals by geological locale—an assignment that required undeniably more exertion to do physically. With a propelled announcing instrument, the exertion required to make such a report diminishes altogether. Now and again, business intelligence instruments can robotize the announcing procedure totally.

Joint Effort

Joint effort highlights enable clients to work over similar data and same records together progressively and are currently extremely normal in present-day business intelligence stages. Cross-gadget cooperation will keep on driving the advancement of better than ever business intelligence apparatuses. A coordinated effort in BI stages can be significant when making new reports or dashboards.

For instance, the CEO of an innovation organization may need a customized report or dashboard of spotlight bunch data on another item inside 24 hours. Item administrators, data examiners, and QA analyzers could all at the same time manufacture their particular segments of the report or dashboard to finish it on time with a communitarian BI apparatus.

Business Intelligence Best Practices

Business intelligence activities can possibly succeed if the association is submitted and executes it deliberately. Basic variables include:

Business Sponsorship

Business sponsorship is the most significant achievement factor on the grounds that even the most ideal framework can't defeat an absence of business responsibility. In the event that the association can't think of the financial limit for the undertaking or officials are occupied with non-BI activities, the task can't be fruitful.

Business Needs

It's essential to comprehend the requirements of the business to properly actualize a business intelligence framework. This comprehension is twofold—both end clients and IT offices have significant needs, and they regularly vary. To pick up this basic comprehension of BI necessities, the association must break down all the different needs of its constituents.

Sum and Quality of the Data

A business intelligence activity may be effective on the off chance that it fuses excellent data at scale. Basic data sources incorporate customer relationships with the board (CRM) programming, sensors, promoting stages, and venture asset arranging (ERP) apparatuses. Poor data will prompt poor choices, so data quality is significant.

A typical procedure to deal with the nature of data will be data profiling, where data is inspected and statistics are gathered for improved data administration. It looks after consistency, diminishes hazard, and streamlines search through metadata.

Client Experience

Consistent client experience is basic with regards to business intelligence since it can advance client appropriation and, at last, drive more an incentive from BI items and activities. End client reception will be a battle without a legitimate and usable interface.

Data Gathering and Cleansing

Data can be assembled from a vast number of sources and can without much of a stretch overpower an association. To anticipate this and make an incentive with business intelligence ventures, associations must distinguish basic data. Business intelligence data frequently incorporates CRM data, contender data, industry data, and that's just the beginning.

Undertaking Management

One of the most fundamental fixings to solid task the board is opening essential lines of correspondence between undertaking staff, IT, and end clients.

Getting Buy-In

There are various sorts of purchases in, and it's vital from top chiefs when obtaining another business intelligence item. Experts can get purchase in from IT by imparting IT inclinations and requirements. End clients have necessities and inclinations too, with various prerequisites.

Prerequisites Gathering

Prerequisites social occasion is seemingly the most significant best practice to pursue, as it takes into consideration more straightforwardness when a few BI devices are up for examination. Necessities originate from a few constituent gatherings, including IT and business clients.

Preparing

Preparing drives end client selection. In the event that end, clients aren't properly prepared, appropriation and worth creation become much increasingly slow to accomplish. Numerous business intelligence suppliers, including MicroStrategy, give instruction administrations, which can consist of preparing and accreditations for all related clients. Preparing can accommodate any key gathering related to a business intelligence venture.

Support

Support engineers, regularly gave by business intelligence suppliers, address specialized issues inside the product or administration. Get familiar with MicroStrategy's support contributions.

Others

Organizations ought to guarantee customary BI abilities are set up before the usage of cutting edge analytics, which requires a few key antecedents before it can include esteem. For instance, data purging must, as of now, be brilliant and framework models must be set up.

BI apparatuses can likewise be a black-box to numerous clients, so it's essential to persistently approve their yields. Setting up an input framework for mentioning and executing client mentioned changes is significant for driving constant improvement in business intelligence.

Functions of Business Intelligence

Undertaking Reporting

One of the key elements of business intelligence is undertaking to detail the ordinary or specially appointed arrangement of significant business data to key inside partners. Reports can take numerous structures and can be delivered, utilizing a few techniques. Be that as it may, business intelligence items can computerize this procedure or straightforwardness agony focuses on reportage, and BI items can empower undertaking level scalability in report creation.

OLAP

Online systematic processing (OLAP) is a way to deal with taking care of expository issues with different measurements. It is a branch of online exchange processing (OLTP). The key an incentive in OLAP is this multidimensional angle, which enables clients to take a gander at issues from an assortment of points of view. OLAP can be utilized to finish assignments, for example, CRM data analysis, monetary forecasting, planning, and others.

Analytics

Analytics is the way toward examining data and drawing out examples or patterns to settle on key choices. It can help reveal shrouded designs in data. Analytics can be unmistakable, prescriptive, or predictive. Illustrative analytics portray a dataset through proportions of focal inclination (mean, middle, mode) and spread (extend, standard deviation, and so on).

Prescriptive analytics is a subset of business intelligence that endorses explicit activities to upgrade results. It decides a reasonable game-plan dependent on data. Along these lines, prescriptive analytics is circumstance ward, and arrangements or models ought not to be summed up to various use cases.

Predictive analytics, otherwise called predictive analysis or predictive modeling, is the utilization of factual methods to make models that can anticipate future or obscure occasions. Predictive analytics is an incredible asset to forecast slants inside a business, industry, or on an increasingly large scale level.

Procedure Mining

Procedure mining is an arrangement of a database where best in class calculations are applied to datasets to uncover designs in the data. Procedure mining can be applied to a wide range of kinds of data, including organized and unstructured data.

Benchmarking

Benchmarking is the utilization of industry KPIs to gauge the accomplishment of a business, a venture, or a procedure. It is a key action in the BI biological system and generally utilized in the business world to make steady upgrades to a business.

Smart Enterprise

The above are altogether unmistakable objectives or elements of business intelligence, yet BI is most important when its applications move past customary choice support frameworks (DSS). The approach of distributed computing and the blast of cell phones implies that business clients request analytics anytime and anyplace—so portable BI has now turned out to be basic to business achievement.

At the point when a business intelligence arrangement comes to far and wide in an association's technique and activities, it can utilize its data, individuals, and venture resources in manners that weren't conceivable previously—it can turn into an intelligent enterprise. Get familiar with how MicroStrategy can enable your association to turn into an intelligent enterprise.

Key Challenges of Business Intelligence

Unstructured Data

To take care of issues with accessibility and data appraisal, it's important to know something about the substance. At present, business intelligence frameworks and technologies expect data to be organized enough to safeguard accessibility and data evaluation. This organizing should be possible by including setting with metadata.

Numerous associations likewise battle with data quality issues. Indeed, even with perfect BI engineering and frameworks, organizations that have sketchy or deficient data will battle to get purchase in from clients who don't confide in the numbers before them.

Poor Adoption

Numerous BI tasks endeavor to altogether supplant old apparatuses and systems, yet this frequently brings about poor client appropriation, with clients returning to the instruments and procedures they're all right with. Numerous specialists propose that BI undertakings come up short on account of the time it takes to make or run reports, which makes clients more averse to receive new technologies and bound to return to inheritance devices.

Another purpose behind business intelligence venture disappointment is lacking client or IT preparation. Lacking preparing can prompt disappointment and overpower, damning the venture.

Absence of Stakeholder Communication

Inside correspondence is another key factor that can spell disappointment for business intelligence ventures. One potential trap is giving false want to clients during usage. BI activities are sometimes charged as convenient solutions, however, they regularly transform into enormous and upsetting undertakings for everybody included.

Absence of correspondence between end clients and IT offices can take away from venture achievement. Necessities from IT and buyers ought to line up with the requirements of the group of end clients. On the off chance that they don't work together, the last item may not line up with desires and needs, which can cause dissatisfaction from all gatherings and a bombed venture. Fruitful activities give business clients important apparatuses that additionally meet inward IT necessities.

Wrong Planning

The exploration and warning firm Gartner cautions against one-quit looking for business intelligence items. Business intelligence items are profoundly separated, and it's significant that customers discover the item that suits their association's requirements for capacities and evaluating.

Associations sometimes treat business intelligence as a series of activities rather than a liquid procedure. Clients regularly solicit changes on a continuous premise, so having a procedure for reviewing and actualizing enhancements is basic.

CHAPTER 8:

Data Mining

D ata mining is a trendy field in machine technology. The
concept was first generated in the 90s. The idea of data
mining has been, from a broad perspective, referred to as
big data or data science. The definition of this concept varies
depending on the application and scope.

Thanks to the advancement in computer networks, data can now be
stored effectively and cheaply. Additionally, the transfer of data has
been enhanced due to the availability of electronic sources. These
reasons and many more have enabled the spread of data mining
techniques. Many organizations are thereby able to store massive

amounts of data in databases without the fear of losing sensitive information.

The ability to store vast amounts of data in databases is excellent. However, it is also essential to know how to analyze and interpret the sets of data at your disposal. Possessing larges sets of data that we cannot explain and draw meaningful information from is as good as having no data at all. That brings the question of how to analyze data stored in various databases. Traditional methods of analyzing data included the manual hand analysis process. However, conventional methods have proved to be time-consuming, tedious, and the result may not reflect accurate outcomes. The traditional ways missed critical information in datasets making the analysis processes a miss.

Additionally, the emergence of massive sets of data has made conventional techniques irrelevant and unrealistic. To mitigate the problems, automated methods have been designed to help sort data and extract useful information, trends, and patterns that may be desirable. The field is where data mining methods and techniques come in handy.

In clear terms, data mining processes aim at explaining the outcome of an event, forecasting future results, and helping in understanding complex data. The science of data mining has been used to describe phenomena such as why a ship sank or plane crushed. In airplanes, data mining is done through black boxes that fit with datasets and information about every flight. This way, it's easy to tell the circumstances that led to a crush. As opposed to other machine learning methods of predicting outcomes, data mining techniques are used to foretell the possible outcome based on facts and not instinct.

The Process for Analyzing Data

For an efficient means of data mining, there must be an observance of seven steps called the knowledge discovery in databases. The seven stages of knowledge discovery in databases are illustrated below.

Data cleaning. This is the first step in analyzing data. In this phase, data is cleaned to remove noise and other variations that may hamper proper analysis.

Data integration. The second step following data cleaning is data integration. This process involves linking, infusing, and incorporating data from various sources to prepare the data that is to be analyzed. For instance, if the information is stored in different databases, integration is done to put the data together in one database.

Data selection. After data is put together in a single file, the relevant set is chosen for analysis. This is a process called data selection.

Data transformation. Having done all the procedures above, the data is now ready to be converted into a fitting format. The conversion is done to make analysis easy. For instance, some techniques of mining data may require that all arithmetic values be standardized.

Data mining. This step involves the application of data mining algorithms to analyze the data and extract meaningful patterns and information from the analyzed sets of data.

Assessment of the extracted patterns and knowledge. This step in data mining involves the study and evaluation of the derived patterns and information from the analyzed data. The review of results can be done in subjective or objective terms.

Visualization of data. The last step in the data mining process is the conception of the extracted information from the analyzed data. This step is when we try to understand the outcome.

It is essential to know that the steps above may vary depending on the technique and the algorithms used. For instance, some algorithms of data mining may perform the steps concurrently or continuously.

Application of Data Mining in Related Fields

Several data mining algorithms can be used in the various sectors and domains where data analysis is vital. Some of these applications are listed below.

- Detection of fraud
- Prediction of stock market valuations
- Analyzing the purchasing patterns of clients

In a broad sense, the techniques of data mining are chosen based on the following metrics.

- The type of data to be analyzed
- The form in which the information extracted from datasets is required.

- The application of extracted knowledge (how the information is used)

Relationship Between Data Mining and Other Research Areas

Data mining is an inter-categorical field of study that overlaps and corresponds to different segments such as machine learning, computer science, soft computing, etc. The relationship between data mining and these fields overlay the fundamental notion of supplementing artificial intelligence. This notion holds that each subsect and area in artificial intelligence complement each other and work both dependently and independently.

Data Mining and Statistics

There are striking differences between data mining and statistics. However, the two fields of research have many components and concepts in common.

In the past, descriptive statistics concentrated on labeling data using metrics, while inferential statistics put more weight on theory analysis to draw noteworthy inference from the data or generate prototypes. On the contrary, data mining techniques are more concerned about the outcome of the study as opposed to arithmetical implication. Many methods of data mining do not focus on the arithmetic test or connotation, as long as given metrics like viability and precision are met to the maximum. Additionally, data mining is usually concentrated on automated analysis of datasets, and in most cases, by machinery that can scale to a massive amount of data. The proximity in scope is realized by mathematicians, who sometimes refer to data mining in statistics as "statistical learning."

Main Data Mining Software

To successfully perform the process of data mining, there are some software and algorithmic computer program available. The software varies in model and use. Some software is all-purpose implements that offer algorithms of different kinds, other software is more specified. It is important to note that some software is developed for commercial purposes, while others are free to access and configure (open-source). The various software can perform data mining on several data types.

Data mining software and algorithms are specifically developed to be used on different types of data. Below, I offer a summary of the countless examples of data generally bumped into, and which can be analyzed using the methods of data mining.

Relational databases: relational databases are the classic type of database that is mostly found in institutions and firms. In this form, data is categorically structured in tables. Conventional methods, like SQL, are used to query the database when trying to find faster information in the database. However, data mining enables the finding of sophisticated patterns within the database.

Customer transaction databases: another commonly used type of database is the customer transaction database. This type is mostly used in retail stores. The database is made up of all dealings made by the clients.

The study of this database is essential in understanding the patterns of purchase and sales. It allows the retailers to understand the changes in the market, thus helping in planning sales and marketing strategies.

Temporal data: Another prevalent form of data is temporal data. The mundane type considers the time dimension in the data. Here, arrangements are created in many realms such as a sequence of items purchased by a customer, a chain of part of the population that is vegan, etc. The temporal data is further divided into time series. The series is a systematic list of arithmetic values, like the price of shares in the stock market.

Spatial data: another set of data that can be easily analyzed is spatial data. This type of data consists of aggregate information like environmental data, forestry data, and data about substructures such as railway lines and air distribution channels.

Spatio-temporal data: this is a type of data that has both characteristics of spatial and temporal data. For instance, the data can be about climatic conditions, the movement of the wilder beast in crowds, etc.

Text data: the text type of data has become a widely studied area in data mining. The utilization spreads even though text data is mostly amorphous. Text documents are mostly disorganized and lack a definite form. Examples of text data are in feeling analysis and composition acknowledgment (predicting the author of a given text).

Web data: this a type of data that originates from websites. The data is mainly sets of a document, e.g., journals from the web with attached links. The sets are bound to form a graph. Some specific examples of data mining activities on the internet include predicting the possible next page on the website, grouping the webpages according to subjects automatically, and evaluating the time taken on every webpage.

Graph data: graphs are also another type of database. Charts are found in social networks (for instance, the list of Facebook friends) and chemistry (for example, a graph of biochemical molecules and atoms).

Assorted data. Different or miscellaneous type of data is a collection of many kinds of data. The classes are linked and can be sorted into a specific arrangement.

Data streams: A data stream is said to be a continuous and high-speed torrent of data that is theoretically boundless. For instance, the data stream can be ecological data, data from video cameras, or digital television data). The limitation of this type of data is that it cannot be adequately stored in the computer. Therefore, the data should be evaluated regularly using suitable methods of data mining. Everyday data mining tasks in stream data are usually the detection of variations and tendencies.

Patterns Found in Data

As deliberated, the objective of data mining is to mine desirable patterns of information from data. The leading types of designs that can be extracted from data are as follows (take note that this list is not the finished product):

Clusters

Algorithms used for clustering are always applied in a situation where the sets of data are supposed to be sort in groups of similar instances (clusters). The main aim of these algorithms is condensing data to make it easy to understand and make an inference. Clustering modus operandi likes K-Means can be utilized to robotically group student showing similar performance.

Classification Models

The algorithms used for classification tasks are purposed to extract models, which can be used to group objects and new instances into classes. For example, classification algorithms such as Naïve Bayes, decision trees, and the neural networks can be used to create designs capable of predicting the trends in customer behaviors or the possibility of individual students to pass an examination. These models can also be hauled out to execute a forecast about the future.

Patterns and Associations

Some methods are designed to study the relationship between data and frequently occurring patterns. For instance, the frequency of an item set can be analyzed, using data mining algorithms, to determine the most purchased items in particular retail outlets. Additional types of patterns are temporal patterns, progressive rules, irregular patterns, and recurrent subgraphs.

Anomaly Detection

The AD is a method of machine learning that seeks to detect glitches and variances within a given set of data.

CHAPTER 9:

Machine Learning and
How It Fits With Data Science

Machine learning can definitely be an important part of the data science process, as long as we use it properly.

Remember, as we go through this process, that part of data science is working on data analysis. This helps us to take a lot of the data we have collected along the way, and then actually see the insights and the predictions that are inside of it. To make this happen, we need to be able to create our models (that can sort through all of the data), find the hidden patterns, and provide us with our insights.

To define these models, and to make sure that they work the way that we want, we need to have a variety of good algorithms in place, and this is where machine learning is going to come into play quite a bit. You will find that with the help of machine learning, and the variety of algorithms that are present in machine learning, we can create models that can go through any kind of data we have, whether it is big or small, and provide us with the answers that we need here.

Machine learning is a process that we can use to make the system or the machine we are working with think in a manner that humans do.

This allows the algorithm to go through and find hidden patterns in the same manner that a human would be able to do, but it can do it much faster and more efficiently than any human could do manually.

Think about how hard this would be to do manually for any human, or even for a group of people who are trying to get through all of that data. It could take them years to get through all of that data and find the insights that they need. And with how fast data are being generated and collected, those predictions and insights would be worthless by the time we got to that point anyway.

Machine learning can make this process so much easier. It allows us to have a way to think through the data and find the hidden patterns and insights that are inside for our needs. With the right machine learning algorithm, we can learn how the process works, and all of the steps that are necessary to make this happen for us. With this in mind, it is time to take a closer look at machine learning, and all of the parts that we need to know to make this work for our needs.

What Is Machine Learning?

The first thing that we need to take a look at here is the basics of machine learning. Machine learning is going to be one of the applications of artificial intelligence that can provide a system with the ability to learn, all on its own, without the help of a programmer telling the system what to do. The system can even take this a bit further and can work to improve based on its own experience, and none of this is done with the system being explicitly programmed in the process. The idea of machine learning is going to be done with a focus on the development of programs on the computer that can access any data you have, and can then use that presented data to learn something new, and how you would like it to behave.

There are going to be a few different applications that we can look at when it comes to using machine learning. As we start to explore more about what machine learning can do, you may notice that over the years, it has been able to change and develop into something that programmers are going to enjoy working with more than ever. When you want to make your machine or system does a lot of the work on its own, without you having to step in and program every step, then machine learning is the right option for you.

When it comes to the world of technology, we will find that machine learning is pretty unique and can add to a level of fun to the coding that we do. There are already a lot of companies, in a variety of industries (which we will talk about in a bit), that will use machine learning and are already receiving a ton of benefits from it.

There are a lot of different applications when it comes to using machine learning, and it is amazing what all we can do with this kind of artificial intelligence. Some of the best methods that we can follow and focus our time on when it comes to machine learning include:

Research on statistics: Machine learning is already making some headway when it comes to the world of IT. You will find that machine learning can help you go through a ton of complex data, looking for the large and important patterns that are in the data. Some of the different applications of machine learning under this category will include things like spam filtering, credit cards, and search engines.

An analysis of big data: There are a lot of companies who have spent time collecting what is known as big data, and now they have to find a way to sort through and learn from that data, in a short amount of time. Companies can use these data to learn more about how money is spent by the customers, and even to help them make important decisions about the future. If we had someone go through and manually do the work, it would take much too long. But with machine learning, we can get it all done. Options like the medical field, election campaigns, and even retail stores have started to turn to Machine Learning to gain some of these benefits.

The financial world: Many financial companies have been able to rely on machine learning. Stock trading online, for example, will rely on this kind of work, and we will find that machine learning can help with fraud detection, loan approvals, and more.

To help us get going with this one, and to understand how we can receive the value that we want out of machine learning, we have to make sure that we pair the best algorithms with the right processes and tools. If you are using the wrong kind of algorithm to sort through these data, you are going to get a lot of inaccurate information, and the results will not give you the help that you need. Working with the right algorithm, the whole time will make a big difference.

The cool thing that we will see with this one is that there is a lot of machine learning algorithms that we can choose from at this point to work on your model. Each of these works in a different manner than the others, but this ensures that you can handle any kind of problem that comes along with your project. With this in mind, though, you will notice that some of the different available algorithms include random forests, neural networks, clustering, support vector machines, and more.

As we are working on some of the models that we want to produce, we will also notice that there are a ton of tools and other processes that are available for us to work with. We need to make sure that we pick the right one to ensure that the algorithm and the model that you are working with will perform the way that you would like. The different tools that are available with Machine Learning will include:

- Comprehensive management and data quality.
- Automated ensemble evaluation of the model to help see where the best performers will show up.
- GUIs for helping to build up the models that you want, along with the process flows being built up as well.
- Easy deployment of this so that you can get results that are reliable and repeatable in a quick manner.
- Interactive exploration of the data and even some visualizations that help us to view the information easier.
- A platform that is integrated and end to end to help with the automation of some of the data to the decision process that you would like to follow.

- A tool to compare the different models of machine learning to help us identify the best one to use quickly and efficiently.

CHAPTER 10:

Machine Learning and Business

Machine learning in business also helps improve business scalability, along with improved operations for different companies from around the world. Artificial intelligence tools and machine learning algorithms are designed to perform operations over big data and learn without human intervention. Organizations and businesses can benefit from understanding the need to implement machine learning algorithms in their systems.

Benefits of Machine Learning for the Business World

Machine learning allows businesses to grow and prosper by effectively analyzing big data, user trends, and market scenarios. Because algorithms extract meaningful insights to solve complex and data-rich business problems with raw data, algorithms have the ability to learn iteratively from data and computers can discover different categories of hidden insights without being explicitly programmed. Machine learning models and algorithms have become extremely popular in the business analytics community to take into account factors such as growing amounts of data.

With the increasing data level, companies are now taking advantage of machine learning and artificial intelligence models to manage operations and everyday tasks, without the need to regularly update the systems, big data can be effectively handled by machine learning algorithms because they are designed to learn through experience.

Finance, economics, education, transportation, healthcare, and medicine industries have now updated their systems with the latest machine learning models to automate processes for accurate results.

The Effects of Machine Learning

Machine learning has revolutionized the operation and performance of systems used in our daily lives. From automation to accurate prediction, artificial intelligence and machine learning models can perform specific tasks without human intervention. The operation and functionality of systems in various industries have now completely changed since machines have been programmed to operate independently.

We notice that the need for human labor is decreasing every day, which is a big problem to consider. While machine learning has amazing benefits in our daily lives, it has affected the jobs of thousands of people. The need for human resources has been largely eliminated through the implementation of automated machines programmed to work and learn independently. On the other hand, while the cost of setting up machine learning and artificial intelligence models on new systems is higher, it certainly brings more benefits to industries in the long run.

Each technology has some drawbacks, along with the benefits, and this is no different from machine learning and artificial intelligence technologies. Machine learning engineers are in high demand due to the ever-increasing data in systems. Artificial intelligence is everywhere, and we may somehow use it without knowing it. Machine learning is modeled in computers and software because devices can work through cognition and work the same way as the human brain.

Today, companies focus on machine learning to improve business decisions and also increase productivity. With the exponential growth of technology, we need better tools to analyze and understand the data we receive and also to prepare our systems for the increasing data or big data in the coming years.

Considerations and Implications

The level of intelligence that a machine exercises is known as the moral component and is a direct result of the data received. Based on the input data, machines can train themselves to work in a certain direction and even against the interest of some people. Scientists and researchers are still unable to remove biases from a machine learning algorithm that can yield results that are not suitable for a politically correct society. In addition, researchers, experts, and scientists believe that artificial intelligence is harmful to society as it can be developed to reflect the human brain and all its prejudices.

Risk assessment accuracy is another significant aspect of machine learning algorithms. Risk assessments are used to measure and evaluate potential risks that may be involved in specific scenarios, and allowing artificial intelligence to make important decisions on behalf of people can increase trust between people and machines.

The advocates of creating transparency in applying for artificial intelligence to create a regulated and shared database that is not owned by a single authority with the power to manipulate data. Algorithm transparency will also help create a high level of trust between users and machines.

Risks Associated With Machine Learning

While machine learning models are very accurate and make accurate predictions, there are some risks associated with intelligent machines that can produce negative results for humans. Machines can surpass the highest level of intelligence to a point where they can psychologically manipulate humans and become destructive to humans. Usually, people cannot align the goals of artificial intelligence with the values of humanity, allowing machines to make decisions that are not achievable by humans.

Machines that perform multiple operations on large amounts of unrelated big data find correlations and patterns that are meaningless at best and wrong at worst. In the long run, machines even train themselves on faulty inputs, teaching them to make future decisions that are not for human benefit. Machine learning risks are real and can prove very dangerous if not properly managed.

Data, design, and output are the three main categories of machine learning that are directly related to risk. Bias, data, lack of model variability, and output interpretation are the main risks that can arise during machine learning operations.

When learning and making predictions, machine learning models can be biased and make inaccurate predictions. Since it mainly depends on data entry, having insufficient data, or having incorrect data can also pose enormous risks to the modeling process. In addition, a lack of model variability and output interpretation can also pose a huge risk to people if the models are not properly trained.

Preventing Bias in Machine Learning

Self-correction is the primary focus of the artificial intelligence industry as researchers find new ways to strengthen ethics and reduce bias in rule-based artificial systems. Taking into account human biases, there are several important aspects of ethics in artificial intelligence to work on. Here are some of the best ways to avoid bias when designing machine learning and artificial intelligence models:

- Selecting the right learning model: Not all artificial intelligence models are suitable for every task. Since each problem requires a specific solution and requires different data sources, there is no proven way to avoid bias. To solve this problem, machine learning models must be designed with parameters best suited to the industry where the system will be deployed. In addition, informing the development team in advance can help companies and industries to use the most appropriate machine learning models.

Supervised and unsupervised machine learning models have their own advantages and disadvantages. The supervised models provide greater control over bias in data selection, while the unattended models that perform dimensional reduction have the ability to take bias out of their data set. Data scientists must identify and present the best model for a specific situation so that effective strategies can be implemented for long-term benefit.

- Choose the training data set: Artificial intelligence and machine learning models learn from the data input. Thus, to obtain accurate and secure predictions, data scientists are required to provide the AI models with data of different types and exclude any vulnerabilities. Training algorithms are done to avoid bias in data selection, for which we need to ensure that training data is diverse. If there is insufficient data for a group, the weighting approach can be used to increase effectiveness on training, but this should be done with extreme care.

- Monitor performance through real data: Discriminatory models usually operate in controlled environments, and no company consciously creates biased artificial intelligence models. Unfortunately, test groups are used to check algorithms that are already in production and that pose future problems. Using statistical methods instead of real data is a better approach for monitoring performance through real data, because when looking for equality, we need to examine data for equality of outcome and equal opportunities.

While it is difficult to prove the equality of opportunity, testing and monitoring machine learning models in the real world can certainly help researchers develop highly accurate models and algorithms. For self-learning systems, using biased data to feed the models can sometimes lead to unintended and dangerous results.

Conclusion

Machine learning is becoming more and more important as time goes by. This is an exciting time to enter computer science and data science and learn how to use these tools in order to complete amazing tasks. Although machine learning seems brand new, the concept of machines and learning goes back to the dawn of time. Human beings have always been tool makers and tool users, and today's machine learning systems and artificial intelligence are merely the latest 'iteration' in the long history of humans extending their minds through the use of tools.

And that is an important concept. Unfortunately, these days there is a lot of fear-mongering regarding artificial intelligence. People seem to be vulnerable to the same old fantasies even if the empirical evidence says otherwise. The Luddites were wrong, the machines actually created 10 – 100 more jobs than they eliminated. Machines free up people to engage in more productive activities, and when productivity is increased jobs, activities, and opportunities increase as well.

The same holds true today, as it always has. Each new generation brings up the old Luddite ideas, only to see them die yet again. This happened in the early 1980s when the invention of spreadsheets and accounting programs on personal computers led people to a state of fear where they imagined accountants and office workers would no longer be necessary. Then they did the same thing with word processors, imagining that secretarial work would be eliminated. Neither happened.

Now here we are again. After languishing for decades, artificial intelligence is finally coming to life. Robotics is enhancing the capability of manufacturing companies to produce more output with less cost and labor. Despite the fact that as I am writing this, the economy is at full employment, politicians and people in the media are once again making the Luddite charge. This time artificial intelligence and machine learning are coming for your jobs. The short-sighted people who promote these fears miss the point entirely, they fail to see that the changes the world is currently going through are going to do what they always have and that raises productivity and free people to do other things.

Hopefully, they won't stop this exciting engine. I suspect they won't be able to. Governments and corporations are already in love with machine learning. The reason is simple. Machine learning works. After decades of oversold promises, computers are now in a position where they can learn, and once trained, they work autonomously. Machine learning makes corporations run more efficiently and helps the government identify fraud, prevent cyberattacks, and do a million other things. Since intelligence is general, the applications of machine learning and AI are general.

AI holds out a special fear for people who hold the Luddite perspective. It's one thing to say that a machine is going to destroy your job, but people also have unrealistic fears of machine learning systems. They seem to think that AI and robots are going to take over the world as if they are living in some kind of science fiction fantasy. There is no doubt that as the years go by, machine learning is going to continue to improve and be able to take on more tasks, but what those tasks are used for is entirely in human control.

These tools can be used for nefarious purposes. In the Republic of China, machine learning tools like facial recognition are being used to control and harass people. Tools that in the United States and Europe are used to determine someone's creditworthiness for a loan are being used in China to give people a 'social score.' According to news reports, the social score can be used to keep people from traveling or being able to leave the country.

So there is no question that in the wrong hands, the tools of machine learning can be used with bad intent. But that has nothing to do with the tools themselves and this kind of situation applies to any technology that human begins have ever invented. We can't control what everyone does in other countries, but we can control how the tools are used here. Each of us has a responsibility to do this. If the government misuses these tools, then they need to be called out for doing so and you should vote for politicians who will manage AI in an ethical fashion. With private companies, that task is easier, simply avoid any private company that uses them in an unethical fashion.

At this point, I'd like to personally thank every reader for taking the time to read and making it all the way to the end. If you are new to machine learning, my hope is that you've come away with some of the mystery behind it stripped away. It's not as complicated as it might seem when you are first exposed to the ideas, or just hearing about them in the media.

If you are really interested in machine learning and would like to become educated in it and possibly pursue it as a career, the best place to start is to learn how to code. In order to get a job in this competitive field, you are probably going to need some kind of academic degree and this is one of the few areas in college where you can go to school and directly learn the skills you are going to need on the job. But you can get started by learning python, which is a simple programming language that runs on any system. You can get online and search for machine learning algorithms built in python that can use small data sets to start giving you practice in this field.

If you decide to go further, my advice is to either major in statistics or computer science, or ideally double-major in computer science and mathematics. Studying computer science alone is probably inadequate because you need to have an advanced grasp of probability and statistics in order to actually pursue a career in data science.

I would also recommend taking a few business courses. You will want to learn about things like logistics, where data science is often applied to generate solutions for large corporations. It works well and I can guarantee that one thing you will be able to count on is you will be able to get a job doing this if you get the right education.

How far you go is up to you, the more education, the higher level at which you are going to start and these types of fields can be very competitive. A master's degree would be great and for those who want it, a Ph.D. will put them in the best position. If you have followed my advice with a double major, you can pick one or the other for a master's degree; it's not necessary to continue trying to get more academic credentials in both.

Working with machine learning is a different type of activity than traditional computer programming. Of course, traditional computer programming is still around and alive and well, so let's not kill it off yet.

www.ingramcontent.com/pod-product-compliance
Lightning Source LLC
LaVergne TN
LVHW051744050326
832903LV00029B/2706